LOS GATOS LIBRARY
LOS GATOS, CALIFORNIA

LOS GATOS LIBRARY

LOS GATOS, CALIFORNIA

FOOD & NATURAL RESOURCES

Exploring Career Pathways

Diane Lindsey Reeves

HELLO WORLD OF WORK

This is you.

Right now, your job is to go to school and learn all you can.

This is the world of work.

It's where people earn a living, find purpose in their lives, and make the world a better place.

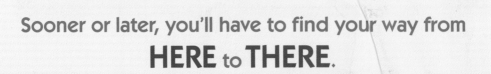

Sooner or later, you'll have to find your way from

HERE to THERE.

To get started, take all the jobs in the incredibly enormous world of work and organize them into an imaginary pile. It's a big pile, isn't it? It would be pretty tricky to find the perfect job for you among so many options.

No worries!

Some very smart career experts have made it easier to figure out. They sorted jobs and industries into groups by the types of skills and products they share. These groups are called career clusters. They provide pathways that will make it easier for you to find career options that match your interests.

Architecture & Construction   Human Services

Arts & Communications   Information Technology

Business & Administration   Law & Public Safety

Education & Training   Manufacturing

Finance   Marketing

Food & Natural Resources   Science, Technology, Engineering & Mathematics (STEM)

Government

Health Sciences   Transportation

Hospitality & Tourism

Good thing you are still a kid.

You have lots of time to explore ideas and imagine yourself doing all kinds of amazing things. The **World of Work** (WoW for short) series of books will help you get started.

TAKE A HIKE!

There are 16 career pathways waiting for you to explore. The only question is: Which one should you explore first?

Is **Food and Natural Resources** a good path for you to start exploring career ideas? There is a lot to like about careers in **food** and **natural resources**. The entire human race would be in big trouble if there weren't people in these fields. We all depend on these workers for things that sustain life—food, water, energy, and more.

See if any of the following questions grab your interest.

WOULD YOU ENJOY exploring nature, growing your own garden, or setting up a recycling center at your school?

CAN YOU IMAGINE someday working at a national park, raising crops in a city farm, or studying food in a laboratory?

ARE YOU CURIOUS ABOUT what landscape architects, chefs, food scientists, environmental engineers, or forest rangers do?

If so, it's time to take a hike! Keep reading to see what kinds of opportunities you can discover along the Food and Natural Resources pathway.

But wait!

What if you don't think you'll like this pathway?

You have two choices.

You could keep reading, to find out more than you already know. You might be surprised to learn how many amazing careers you'll find along this path.

OR

Turn to page 27 to get ideas about other WoW pathways.

ANIMAL TRAINER

ENVIRONMENTAL ENGINEER

LANDSCAPE ARCHITECT

FOREST RANGER

FOOD SCIENTIST

WoW Up Close

Feeding the world. Protecting the environment. Taking care of wildlife. Finding ways to use Earth's natural resources wisely. These are just some of the important jobs that people who work along the Food and Natural Resources pathway do.

GREEN ENTREPRENEUR

CHEF

URBAN FARMER

ANIMAL TRAINER

It could be zoo animals. It could be guide dogs, search and rescue dogs, or household pets. It could even be marine mammals in an aquarium. Or, perhaps, horses used for racing, riding, showing, or working.

When it comes to training animals, there are many choices. But people who train animals all share one thing in common: they love the animals they train!

Animal trainers work in kennels, shelters, stables, animal parks, aquariums, pet stores, veterinary clinics, and zoos. Sometimes they work to train animals to behave a little less like, um, animals. This is true of those who train pets to happily coexist with humans. Others train animals to perform, entertain, or compete in races or shows. Still others work to teach animals to do a specific type of job like protect or help humans. These trainers teach dogs to sniff out drugs or bombs or to guide blind people.

Of course, animal trainers need training, too. In some cases, a high school diploma, experience, and special certification can get you started. For other positions, like those found at aquariums or zoos, you'll need a college degree.

Is this the career for you? Your first clue is wanting to spend your spare time with your furry and feathered friends.

Check It Out!

See videos about what it's like to train different kinds of animals at

▶ http://bit.ly/SeaWorldTrainer

▶ http://bit.ly/BuschGardensTrainer

▶ http://bit.ly/HorseTrainer

▶ http://bit.ly/MilitaryDogTrainer

Start Now!

✔ Take care of a pet (with permission, of course!).

✔ Volunteer to help out at a local animal shelter.

✔ Become an expert by reading all you can about your favorite animals.

CHEF

What do you like to eat at your favorite restaurant? Chances are, whatever it is, it is made for you by a **chef**. Chefs are professional cooks who work in restaurants. Their job is to plan menus, order food supplies, and manage others on the kitchen staff.

Depending on where they work, one chef might be responsible for feeding hundreds of hungry people in a single night!

Chefs get their start by cooking—at home, in cooking classes, or in after-school jobs at restaurants. They get special training at community colleges or culinary art schools. Then they go out and get as much experience as they can.

Being a chef involves creative talent and lots of hard work. Part of the job involves coming up with delicious new recipes. But most of the job involves preparing those recipes for customers—again and again and again.

Restaurants aren't the only places where chefs work. They may work for airlines, bakeries, catering companies, cruise ships, military bases, resorts, or retirement centers. Some of the very best chefs go on to work in high-end restaurants or write cookbooks. Some even star in their own cooking shows!

It's a delicious career choice for adventurous cooks!

Check It Out!

Find kid-friendly cooking tips and recipes at

▶ http://bit.ly/ FoodNetworkKids

▶ http://bit.ly/ HeyKidsLetsCook

Start Now!

✔ Watch famous chefs in action on the Food Network television channel.

✔ Make a special meal or birthday cake for someone in your family.

✔ See how many different kinds of sandwich recipes you can come up with to pack in your school lunch.

ENVIRONMENTAL ENGINEER

Environmental engineers are problem solvers. They use their knowledge about engineering, biology, chemistry, and other sciences to tackle problems like recycling, waste disposal, public health, and pollution.

Sustainability is a word you hear a lot when it comes to the environment. Sustainability means doing something in a way that doesn't use up natural resources. Environmental engineers might look for sustainable solutions that use solar power instead of energy that is dependent on natural gas or coal. They might research alternative fuel sources for oil. One especially important area that environmental engineers look for sustainable solutions is water supply.

Environmental engineers work to make the world a better place. They develop ways to clean up air pollution caused by factories close to home. They find innovative ways to bring drinkable water to people in faraway countries. They work to fix and prevent problems in earth-friendly ways.

Future environmental engineers need to get started in high school by taking lots of science and math courses, including biology, chemistry, algebra, trigonometry, and calculus. In college, they get degrees that require a mix of classroom, laboratory, and field studies. It takes smart, well-prepared people to solve big problems!

Check It Out!

Watch environmental engineers in action at

▶ http://bit.ly/EnvEngWork

▶ http://bit.ly/EnvironEng

Start Now!

✔ Find creative ways to use thrown-away items found in your family's recycling bin.

✔ Calculate your carbon footprint at http://bit.ly/ZeroFootprintYouth.

✔ Use the Internet to find news about environmental issues in your city.

FOOD SCIENTIST

Thanks to **food scientists**, you can enjoy having cereal for breakfast, a granola bar for lunch, and cookies and milk for an after-school snack. Processed foods like those taste good and last longer in your kitchen pantry because of food scientists.

You may be surprised to learn how much science there is in food science. Chemistry, biology, and cutting-edge **nanotechnology** are used to analyze the nutritional content of foods, create new food products, and uncover ways to keep food safe and healthy. For evidence that science is involved in your favorite packaged food item, just read the ingredients label. All those big words are a sure sign that it is!

Food scientists tend to specialize in certain areas. Some work in laboratories or food test kitchens doing research. Others work for government agencies inspecting food-processing plants. Some work directly with farmers to help them grow stronger, more nutritious crops.

It takes lots of food scientists doing their jobs to keep our food supplies safe and delicious. Food science is a profession that lets you play with your food and eat your experiments, too! Maybe you will be the food scientist who invents a world famous–and healthy–version of fast food burgers and fries!

Check It Out!

See for yourself what it is like to be a food scientist at these websites:

- http://bit.ly/DisneyFoodScientist
- http://bit.ly/IFTFoodScientist
- http://bit.ly/IFTDayinLife

Start Now!

- ✔ Make sure your next science fair project has something to do with food. Here are some fun food science experiments to try at home: http://bit.ly/SteveSpanglerFood.

- ✔ Find information about "food science" or "cooking science" at the library or online. Add the words "for kids" to your search to make it more fun.

FOREST RANGER

What does a **forest ranger** do? A ranger's main job is to protect national forests, the animals that live in them, and the people who visit them. One of the perks of the job is spending workdays in beautiful outdoor spaces.

Rangers get to share their enthusiasm for nature by providing information and education services to visitors.

Daily tasks for forest rangers vary by day and season. Spring may find them planting new tree seedlings, while brutally hot summers may find them involved in fire prevention (or firefighting) activities. They work to keep trails safe and keep an eye out for signs of pests or diseases affecting trees. Sometimes they make lists that show the number and types of trees within the forest. Other times, they may organize search-and-rescue missions to find lost hikers.

In a way, forest rangers are nature's police department. Part of their job is to enforce laws that prevent **poaching**, hunting, **arson**, and **vandalism** on public lands. Bears, wolves, and mountain lions aren't the only potentially dangerous species found in forests!

Park rangers do the same types of tasks in state and national parks, campgrounds, and historic sites enjoyed by millions of visitors every year.

Check It Out!

Only you can prevent wildfires. The famous Smokey Bear has been educating the public about the dangers of forest fires for more than 70 years. Get acquainted with him at

▶ https://smokeybear.com

Start Now!

- ✔ Take a hike and see how many different kinds of trees you can find.

- ✔ Play around with being a WebRanger at https://www. nps.gov/webrangers.

- ✔ Find a national park in your state at https://www.nps. gov/findapark.

GREEN ENTREPRENEUR

Safer playground surfaces made from used automobile tires. Carpets, clothing, automotive parts, and new bottles made from old, empty water bottles. Bicycles made from recycled beverage cans. Recycled paper used to make brand-new paper.

These are just a few of the ways that **green entrepreneurs** make money—and change the world while they are at it. Green entrepreneurs are just like any small (or big!) businessperson. They have an idea for a product and start a business to make and sell the product. The difference is that green entrepreneurs use other people's garbage to make their products.

Like other entrepreneurs, green entrepreneurs juggle many roles. They are the "boss" of their company, and it's up to them to do what it takes for their company to succeed. They hire and manage other employees, make decisions about how their products are produced, and help market and sell their products.

They find creative ways to make products that are earth-friendly and sustainable. Take shoes, for instance. Imagine wearing out a pair made of recycled materials. Instead of tossing them out, you recycle them again. Trash to treasure to trash again!

Check It Out!

Go online to learn about recycling at these fun websites:

▶ http://www.iwanttoberecycled.org/game

▶ https://www3.epa.gov/recyclecity

▶ http://bit.ly/RecycleRoundupGame

Start Now!

✔ Make a list of all the products you can create from recycled plastic bottles.

✔ Use the Internet to investigate what "young green entrepreneurs" are doing around the world.

✔ Create a poster showing how recycling works.

LANDSCAPE ARCHITECT

Have you ever visited a beautiful park or garden? Places like the famous Central Park in New York City and the peaceful Arlington National Cemetery near the nation's capital don't just happen. They are first imagined in the minds and on the drawing boards of **landscape architects**.

Landscape architects design the beautiful outdoor spaces where people live, work, and play. Their work can be enjoyed in public parks, gardens, playgrounds, office complexes, golf courses, neighborhood communities, schools, and other public places. Like the architects who design homes and buildings, landscape architects must earn a college degree, get **internship** experience, and pass a state licensing exam in order to qualify for their jobs.

Landscape architects must know as much about design as they do about plants and trees. They spend much of their time at their design tables. There they use computers to create computer-aided design (CAD) drawings and models of their very detailed plans.

It's up to gardeners and landscapers to do the actual digging and planting. Their work turns a landscape architect's ideas into beautiful spaces that people can enjoy for years to come.

Check It Out!

Explore what landscape architecture is all about at

▶ https://www.asla.org/yourpath/index.html

Start Now!

✔ Sketch out your best ideas for a beautiful recess area for your school.

✔ Use the Internet to find out all you can about Frederick Law Olmsted, the famous landscape architect who designed New York City's Central Park.

✔ Find pictures of favorite plants and flowers and pretty gardens in magazines and online, and use a notebook to organize them.

URBAN FARMER

When you think of a farm, chances are you think of rolling green fields of crops dotted with pastures for cattle and a big red barn. Many times, that's exactly what you'll find when you drive down a country road in an agricultural area.

That's a good thing. Rural and commercial farms provide food for millions of people every year. We would go hungry without them.

Urban **agriculture** is a new kind of farming. Urban gardens are found on smaller plots of land in or near a city. They can also be found in some surprising places, such as abandoned fields in inner-city areas or on skyscraper rooftops. Some **urban farmers** are even experimenting with growing fruits and vegetables inside tall buildings.

The challenge for all urban farmers is to find ways to grow more food in smaller spaces. Some use "hoop houses," which are low-tech greenhouses that make it possible for different crops to grow all year long. This extends the growing season.

The big idea behind urban farming is to grow food closer to where people live. This gives people access to fresh, nutritious food that doesn't have to be transported great distances. It's all about finding earth-friendly and people-friendly solutions! Urban farming is bringing opportunities to farmers around the world.

Check It Out!

Go online to explore topics like

- "history of agriculture"
- "sustainable agriculture"
- "organic farming"

Start Now!

- ✔ Start your own garden at home. All you need are some pots or jars, seeds, and dirt to get started. Add water and sunshine and watch your garden grow!

- ✔ Make a chart showing the differences between a city farm and a country farm.

- ✔ Check into joining a local 4-H club. Find information at http://www.4-h.org.

Agricultural science teacher • Agronomist • Air pollution control engineer • Animal breeder • Animal control expert • Animal nutritionist • Animal scientist • **ANIMAL TRAINER** • Aquaculture director • Aquarist • Aquatic biologist • Arborist • Baker • Biologist • Biology teacher or professor • Botanist • Brand manager • Butcher • Buyer • Certified industrial hygienist • **CHEF** • Chief safety officer • Commercial fisherman • Conservationist • Cook • Cowboy • Crop specialist • Dairy farmer • Dog trainer • Environmental compliance investigator • Environmental analyst • **ENVIRONMENTAL ENGINEER**

WoW Big List

Take a look at some of the different kinds of jobs people do in the Food and Natural Resources pathway. **WoW!**

Some of these job titles will be familiar to you. Others will be so unfamiliar that you will scratch your head and say "huh?"

• Environmental health specialist • Environmental protection specialist • Extension agent • Exterminator • Farm field manager • Farm laborer • Farmer • Finfish aquaculture specialist • Fish and game warden • Fish and wildlife manager • Florist • Food processor • Food safety inspector • **FOOD SCIENTIST** • Food science technician • Food technician • Food technologist • **FOREST RANGER** • Fur trapper • Geologist •

GREEN ENTREPRENEUR • Greenhouse manager • Guide dog trainer • Hatchery manager • Horse trainer • Hunter • Industrial waste inspector • Kennel attendant • Laboratory technician • **LANDSCAPE ARCHITECT** • Landscaper • Licensed veterinary technician • Logger • Meat packer • Merchandiser • Miner • Natural resource officer • Nursery manager • Orchard manager • Park ranger • Pest control operator • Pet Groomer • Procurement manager • Product development manager • Purchasing agent • Quality assurance manager • Rainbow trout farm manager • Rancher • Ranch hand • Recycling Director • Researcher • Risk control

Find a job title that makes you curious. Type the name of the job into your favorite Internet search engine and find out more about the people who have that job.

1 What do they do?

2 Where do they work?

3 How much training do they need to do this job?

consultant • Sales • Sales representative • Sanitary engineer • Science teacher • Science professor • Seed analyst • Service dog trainer • Silviculturist • Soil scientist • Systems ecologist • Transfer station operator • **URBAN FARMER** • Urban forester • Veterinarian • Veterinary assistant • Veterinary nurse • Veterinary surgeon • Waste management specialist • Waste reduction coordinator • Wildlife manager • Zoologist

TAKE YOUR PICK

	Put stars next to your 3 favorite career ideas	Put an X next to the career idea you like the least	Put a question mark next to the career idea you want to learn more about
Animal trainer			
Chef			
Environmental engineer			
Food scientist			
Forest ranger			
Green entrepreneur			
Landscape architect			
Urban farmer			
	What do you like most about these careers?	What is it about this career that doesn't appeal to you?	What do you want to learn about this career? Where can you find answers?

Which Big Wow List ideas are you curious about?

Please do **NOT** write in this book if it doesn't belong to you. You can download a copy of this activity online at www.cherrylakepublishing.com/activities.

EXPLORE SOME MORE

The Food and Natural Resources pathway is only one of 16 career pathways that hold exciting options for your future. Take a look at the other 15 to figure out where to start exploring next.

Architecture and Construction

WOULD YOU ENJOY making things with LEGOs™, building a treehouse or birdhouse, or designing the world's best skate park?

CAN YOU IMAGINE someday working at a construction site, a design firm, or a building company?

ARE YOU CURIOUS ABOUT what civil engineers, demolition technicians, heavy-equipment operators, landscape architects, or urban planners do?

Arts & Communications

WOULD YOU ENJOY drawing your own cartoons, using your smartphone to make a movie, or writing articles for the student newspaper?

CAN YOU IMAGINE someday working at a Hollywood movie studio, a publishing company, or a television news station?

ARE YOU CURIOUS ABOUT what actors, bloggers, graphic designers, museum curators, or writers do?

Business & Administration

WOULD YOU ENJOY playing Monopoly, being the boss of your favorite club or team, or starting your own business?

CAN YOU IMAGINE someday working at a big corporate headquarters, government agency, or international business center?

ARE YOU CURIOUS ABOUT what brand managers, chief executive officers, e-commerce analysts, entrepreneurs, or purchasing agents do?

Education & Training

WOULD YOU ENJOY babysitting, teaching your grandparents how to use a computer, or running a summer camp for neighbor kids in your backyard?

CAN YOU IMAGINE someday working at a college counseling center, corporate training center, or school?

ARE YOU CURIOUS ABOUT what animal trainers, coaches, college professors, guidance counselors, or principals do?

Finance

WOULD YOU ENJOY earning and saving money, being the class treasurer, or playing the stock market game?

CAN YOU IMAGINE someday working at an accounting firm, bank, or Wall Street stock exchange?

ARE YOU CURIOUS ABOUT what accountants, bankers, fraud investigators, property managers, or stockbrokers do?

 ## Government

WOULD YOU ENJOY reading about U.S. presidents, running for student council, or helping a favorite candidate win an election?

CAN YOU IMAGINE someday working at a chamber of commerce, government agency, or law firm?

ARE YOU CURIOUS about what mayors, customs agents, federal special agents, intelligence analysts, or politicians do?

 ## Health Sciences

WOULD YOU ENJOY nursing a sick pet back to health, dissecting animals in a science lab, or helping the school coach run a sports clinic?

CAN YOU IMAGINE someday working at a dental office, hospital, or veterinary clinic?

ARE YOU CURIOUS ABOUT what art therapists, doctors, dentists, pharmacists, and veterinarians do?

 ## Hospitality & Tourism

WOULD YOU ENJOY traveling, sightseeing, or meeting people from other countries?

CAN YOU IMAGINE someday working at a convention center, resort, or travel agency?

ARE YOU CURIOUS ABOUT what convention planners, golf pros, tour guides, resort managers, or wedding planners do?

 ## Human Services

WOULD YOU ENJOY showing a new kid around your school, organizing a neighborhood food drive, or being a peer mediator?

CAN YOU IMAGINE someday working at an elder care center, fitness center, or mental health center?

ARE YOU CURIOUS ABOUT what elder care center directors, hairstylists, personal trainers, psychologists, or religious leaders do?

 ## Information Technology

WOULD YOU ENJOY creating your own video game, setting up a Web site, or building your own computer?

CAN YOU IMAGINE someday working at an information technology start-up company, software design firm, or research and development laboratory?

ARE YOU CURIOUS ABOUT what artificial intelligence scientists, big data analysts, computer forensic investigators, software engineers, or video game designers do?

Law & Public Safety

WOULD YOU ENJOY working on the school safety patrol, participating in a mock court trial at school, or coming up with a fire escape plan for your home?

CAN YOU IMAGINE someday working at a cyber security company, fire station, police department, or prison?

ARE YOU CURIOUS ABOUT what animal control officers, coroners, detectives, firefighters, or park rangers do?

 ## Manufacturing

WOULD YOU ENJOY figuring out how things are made, competing in a robot-building contest, or putting model airplanes together?

CAN YOU IMAGINE someday working at a high-tech manufacturing plant, engineering firm, or global logistics company?

ARE YOU CURIOUS ABOUT what chemical engineers, industrial designers, supply chain managers, robotics technologists, or welders do?

 ## Marketing

WOULD YOU ENJOY keeping up with the latest fashion trends, picking favorite TV commercials during Super Bowl games, or making posters for a favorite school club?

CAN YOU IMAGINE someday working at an advertising agency, corporate marketing department, or retail store?

ARE YOU CURIOUS ABOUT what creative directors, market researchers, media buyers, retail store managers, and social media consultants do?

 ## Science, Technology, Engineering & Mathematics (STEM)

WOULD YOU ENJOY concocting experiments in a science lab, trying out the latest smartphone, or taking advanced math classes?

CAN YOU IMAGINE someday working in a science laboratory, engineering firm, or research and development center?

ARE YOU CURIOUS ABOUT what aeronautical engineers, ecologists, statisticians, oceanographers, or zoologists do?

 ## Transportation

WOULD YOU ENJOY taking pilot or sailing lessons, watching a NASA rocket launch, or helping out in the school carpool lane?

CAN YOU IMAGINE someday working at an airport, mass transit system, or shipping port?

ARE YOU CURIOUS ABOUT what air traffic controllers, flight attendants, logistics planners, surveyors, and traffic engineers do?

MY WoW

I am here.

_____
Name

_____
Grade

_____
School

Who I am.

Make a word collage! Use 5 adjectives to form a picture that describes who you are.

Where I'm going.

The next career pathway I want to explore is

_____

Some things I need to learn first to succeed.

1 _____

2 _____

3 _____

My Career Choice

To get here.

Please do **NOT** write in this book if it doesn't belong to you. You can download a copy of this activity online at www.cherrylakepublishing.com/activities.

GLOSSARY

agriculture
all the jobs involved in growing crops and raising animals to provide food, wool, and other products

animal trainer
a person who teaches animals to do specific jobs, compete in races, entertain people, or simply behave

arson
the crime of setting fire to property with the intention of destroying it

chef
a professional cook in charge of a kitchen in a restaurant

environmental engineer
a person who uses scientific and engineering principles to protect humans and other species from the effects of adverse environmental factors such as pollution

food
all the jobs involved in getting food from the farms that grow it to the people who buy and eat it

food scientist
a person who works to ensure that agricultural establishments are productive and food is safe

forest ranger
a person employed by the government to supervise the care and preservation of forests, especially those found in national, state, and local parks

green entrepreneur
a person who starts a business making products out of other people's garbage products

internship
a position where you can learn a skill or job by working with an expert in that field

landscape architect
a person who designs beautiful outdoor spaces where people live, work, and play

nanotechnology
the art of studying and building devices whose dimensions are extremely small

natural resources
all the jobs involved in using materials produced by the earth that are necessary or useful to people

poaching
hunting or fishing illegally

urban farmer
a person who raises crops on a small plot of land in or near a city

vandalism
the act of damaging or destroying someone else's property

INDEX

* Refers to the Web page sources

About the Author

Diane Lindsey Reeves is the author of lots of children's books. She has written several original PEANUTS stories (published by Regnery Kids and Sourcebooks). She is especially curious about what people do and likes to write books that get kids thinking about all the cool things they can be when they grow up. She lives in Cary, North Carolina, and her favorite thing to do is play with her grandkids—Conrad, Evan, Reid, and Hollis Grace.